D0537070

AMERICA DEBATES ™

AMERICA DEBATES CIVIL LIBERTIES AND TERRORISM

Jeri Freedman

rosen publishing's
rosen
central®

New York

To my niece and nephew, Laura and Matthew Freedman, with love

Published in 2008 by The Rosen Publishing Group, Inc.
29 East 21st Street, New York, NY 10010

Library of Congress Cataloging-in-Publication Data

Freedman, Jeri.
America debates Civil liberties and terrorism / Jeri Freedman—1st ed.
    p. cm.—(America debates)
Includes bibliographical references.
ISBN-13: 978-1-4042-1927-4 (hardcover)
ISBN-10: 1-4042-1927-7 (hardcover)
1. Terrorism—United States—Prevention. 2. Civil rights—United States.
I. Title.
HV6432.F74 2008
323.4'90973—dc22

2007008692

Manufactured in the United States of America

On the cover: Left: A police officer stands guard at the international terminal at Los Angeles International Airport. Right: Demonstrators protest the treatment of terror suspects held at the American detention facility at Guantánamo Bay, Cuba.

CONTENTS

Introduction

Throughout the late twentieth and early twenty-first centuries, hundreds of acts of terrorism have been committed worldwide. In the 1980s and 1990s, foreign terrorists set off bombs at American embassies in Lebanon, Kuwait, Saudi Arabia, Kenya, and Tanzania. In 2000, an American naval ship, the USS *Cole*, was bombed in Yemen. Because these events took place overseas, however, many Americans thought of terrorism as something that occurred far away. On September 11, 2001, this belief was shattered. That day, terrorists used commercial airplanes to attack the World Trade Center in New York and the Pentagon, outside Washington, D.C. Suddenly, Americans felt threatened on their own soil.

In the wake of the terrorist attacks, new laws were quickly passed. The Patriot Act, for example, gave the government broader powers to monitor people's activities and to detain them (lock them up). With the passage of time, however, many came to believe that the powers granted to the government were too broad. These people now fear we have lost some of the important liberties and protections granted by the U.S. Constitution.

Terrorism is not a new phenomenon. Terrorists have been around throughout history, and in countries around the world. But today, terrorists have access to weapons and technology that make it easier for them to attack and harder for law enforcement to detect them. On one hand, law enforcement agencies need access to tools that allow them to track terrorists who are using modern technology. On the other hand, citizens need protection from being pressured or threatened by the government. This book examines the issues involved in trying to balance the need to protect Americans against terrorist attacks with the need to preserve our basic freedoms.

Chapter 1

The New Age of Terror

Before we can explore the issues relating to civil liberties and terrorism, we first must understand what these things are. This chapter takes a closer look at the concepts of terrorism and civil liberties.

WHAT IS TERRORISM?

Terrorism is the use of actual or threatened violence to frighten the public or government of a country to give in to the terrorists' demands. In more official language, the U.S. Department of Defense defines terrorism as "the calculated use of unlawful violence or threat of unlawful violence to inculcate fear; intended to coerce or to intimidate governments or societies in the pursuit of goals that are generally political, religious, or ideological."

THE GOALS OF TERRORISM

Why do people commit terrorist acts? Frequently, they are committed by people who hold strong political or religious views. The following are some of the goals of terrorists:

- **To get publicity for their cause.** Some terrorist leaders think their acts will attract international media attention so they can raise support for their cause.
- **To scare people into demanding that their government give the terrorists what they want.** For example, terrorists may demand withdrawal of troops from an occupied zone or the release of political prisoners.
- **To influence the government directly.** This was the case with the Irish Republican Army (IRA) in the United Kingdom. The IRA used violence—such as setting off bombs under bridges—in an attempt force the British government to give Ireland independence from the U.K.
- **To wage religious jihad.** *Jihad* is an Arabic term meaning "holy war." Some Islamic (Muslim) terrorist groups have encouraged their members to commit terrorist acts as part of a "holy war" against Jews, Christians, and other non-Muslims. Sometimes they commit terrorist acts against the United States and western European countries, which, they claim, aim to spread their corrupt values to Muslim societies.

In 1979, the Irish Republican Army blew up a sailboat carrying Britain's Earl Mountbatten. Above, local Irish youngsters watch a policeman clear away the wreckage.

- **To punish the people of another country by disrupting their lives and reducing their liberty.** Those committing terrorist acts may be motivated by anger or resentment. ("Why should you have a good life, while I'm suffering?" or "Your good life comes at the expense of my poverty.")

Terrorist attacks achieve their effect in two ways:

- **By causing mass panic**, as in the case of the large-scale attack on 9/11.
- **By keeping people from carrying out the activities that allow society to run normally.** Terrorists may do

this by continually making small, apparently random attacks. Their targets are then forced to take constant precautions. This makes it hard to get things done. This technique is used by suicide bombers and others who blow up stores, cafes, hotels, trains, and buses.

WHAT ARE CIVIL LIBERTIES?

"Civil liberties" is a term that describes the legal rights that protect a citizen of a country from unfair treatment by the government. As an American, your civil liberties are guaranteed by the U.S. Constitution.

Terrorist attacks can be so disturbing that we might agree to anything if we think it will keep us safe. We will even accept government activities that reduce our civil liberties. In the long run, however, agreeing to such measures may negatively affect our freedom, and sometimes our lives, just as much as the fear of terrorism.

The founders of the United States lived in dangerous times. They experienced abuse at the hands of government officials charged with "protecting" the colonies. Their homes were searched randomly and without their permission, and their property was taken away by British officials. Soldiers were placed in colonists' houses to keep an eye on them. Speaking out against British policies meant one could be accused of treason (attempting to overthrow the government). The United States' founders also understood that a leader might use a threat posed by a foreign country to convince people to give up their liberties. Taking all of this into consideration, they decided

to write down basic principles for governing the new nation—in the form of the Constitution of the United States.

CONSTITUTIONAL PROTECTIONS

Our freedoms as Americans are spelled out in the Bill of Rights. This document is made up of ten additions, or amendments, to the Constitution. They were added before the original thirteen colonies accepted the Constitution. The amendments most often used to challenge government antiterrorist activities are the First, Fourth, Fifth, Sixth, Seventh, and Eighth Amendments. These relate to free speech, illegal search and seizure, and the conduct of criminal trials.

First Amendment—Freedom of Speech, Press, Religion, and Petition

This amendment states that the government cannot interfere with people's right to practice any religion they choose. It also protects citizens' right to speak freely, gather in groups, and write or speak in the press.

American colonists had few civil liberties under British colonial rule. Government searches, seizures, and violence—such as the bloody Boston Massacre (opposite page)—led to the U.S. Constitution.

A Rhode Island state police officer removes a computer from the home of a suspect. Files and e-mails on computers are excellent sources of evidence regarding a suspect's activities.

Fourth Amendment— Right of Search and Seizure Regulated

This amendment states that people's bodies, houses, papers, and property cannot be searched or taken by the government. The exception is if a representative of the government shows evidence of wrongdoing to a court and gets a warrant, or official authorization. Even then, such a warrant must include the specific place to be searched and what is being searched for.

Fifth Amendment—Provisions Concerning Prosecution

This amendment says that a person can be tried for crime only if a grand jury decides that there is convincing evidence that the person may have committed a crime. The only exception is for people engaged in actual service in times of war or public danger. The Fifth Amendment also protects individuals from making self-incriminating (self-injuring) statements in a court of law. It further states that no one's life, liberty, or property can be taken without a proper trial.

Sixth Amendment—Right to a Speedy Trial, Witnesses, etc.

This amendment states that in all criminal cases, the accused person has the right to a speedy and public trial, by a fair jury. It also states that a person accused of a crime has the right to be informed of what crime he is charged with. The accused is also given the right to see the witnesses against him, to have witnesses speak in his favor, and to have the assistance of a lawyer.

Seventh Amendment—Right to a Trial by Jury

This amendment says that a person accused of a crime will be tried by a jury in a court according to the regular laws of the United States.

Eighth Amendment—Excessive Bail, Cruel Punishment

This amendment says that judges cannot impose unusually large bail (money put up as a guarantee that a person will appear in court). It also says that no cruel and unusual punishments can be applied to people accused of crimes.

In addition to the Bill of Rights, the Constitution outlines a set of "checks and balances" among the three different branches of the government—executive, judicial, and legislative. This is to ensure that no single branch can act by itself in a way that might harm the people.

Chapter 2

The U.S. Government Is Watching

Surveillance is the act of watching and listening to people, usually without their knowledge. One of the aspects of the "War on Terror" that has caused great concern is the government surveillance of American citizens. The issues relating to government surveillance strike at the heart of our most fiercely defended rights to privacy and free speech.

THE PATRIOT ACT

The term "Patriot Act" refers to the Uniting and Strengthening America by Providing Appropriate Tools Required to Intercept and Obstruct Terrorism Act (USA

President George W. Bush looks down at the Patriot Act after signing it into law in a ceremony at the White House on October 26, 2001.

PATRIOT Act) of 2001. It was signed into law by President George W. Bush on October 26, 2001, and it was reauthorized in 2006. The Patriot Act greatly increased the surveillance powers of government law enforcement agencies.

Enhanced Surveillance

The Patriot Act eases restrictions on the use of wiretaps on telephones. In addition, it increases the government's right to gather personal data from electronic communication such as e-mail. The act also increases federal law enforcement agencies' access to an individual's personal financial, credit, educational, medical, and other records. It even allows federal agents to secretly enter people's homes. There, they are allowed to search people's possessions, read and photograph letters and documents, and read and copy files on computers.

Supporters of the Patriot Act claim this type of surveillance is necessary to find evidence that a person is engaged in terrorist activity. People who are more concerned about protecting the rights of Americans fear that such wide-ranging powers allow the government to violate the civil liberties of citizens. They usually claim that the Fourth Amendment of the Bill of Rights forbids such searches.

What Are Gag Orders?

The Patriot Act makes it legal for the government to force people to keep its searches secret. This is called a gag order. Such corporations as phone companies and Internet service providers have been required to turn over all of their customer records. The government has forbidden them to tell their customers about it, and the government says such secrecy is necessary so as not to alert potential terrorists.

People cannot object to these activities if they do not know they are occurring. Obviously, when an individual suspected of a crime is being investigated, that person cannot be told that he or she is under surveillance. In regular criminal cases, a court gives law enforcement agents a warrant, or permission to monitor the activities of a specific person for a limited time. When the investigation is over, however, the person must be told that the surveillance occurred.

Those who object to this type of surveillance say the widespread collection of records of citizens' activities violates the Fourth Amendment. This amendment says that people's property—including records—cannot be searched unless there is evidence that a person is involved in a specific crime. Objectors also say the gag orders violate the First Amendment, which guarantees people's right to free speech.

The People's Right to Know

Gag orders are not the only way of keeping citizens in the dark about the government's activities. Limiting the ability of reporters to cover stories about government activities is another way to keep the activities secret. The First Amendment in the Bill of Rights guarantees the rights of the press to cover important events without government interference. Those writing the Bill of Rights thought this right was so important that they included it in the First Amendment. Since the attacks of 9/11, President George W. Bush and those in his administration have carried on all types of government activities in secret. These include:

- Holding secret congressional hearings about immigration and activities to gather information.
- Holding secret court trials of suspected terrorists.
- Refusing to speak to the press except through formal press conferences, at which they provide only limited information.

All this secrecy makes it hard for citizens to know what the government is doing in their name. (Keep in mind that elected government officials represent the American people.) And it makes it hard for reporters to tell people the real story.

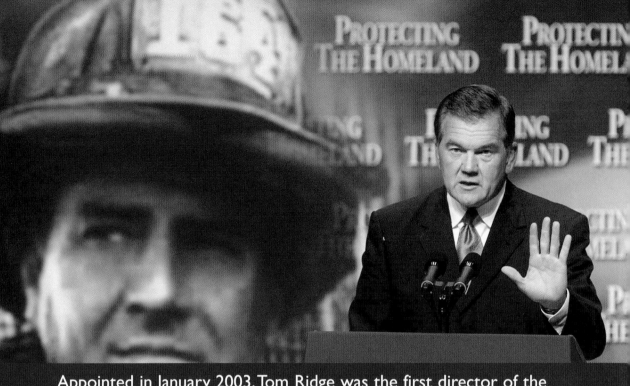

Appointed in January 2003, Tom Ridge was the first director of the U.S. Department of Homeland Security (DHS). The DHS coordinates America's antiterrorism efforts.

On one hand, there is critical information that the government must keep secret. An example is the identity of agents working undercover within terrorist organizations. On the other hand, there is a major problem when the press's access to government officials and information is greatly restricted. Such secrecy makes it very hard for the public to know if the government's activities are helpful or even legal.

LAW ENFORCEMENT OR INTELLIGENCE GATHERING?

Traditionally, law enforcement agents focus on collecting evidence for a specific crime that has already been committed. But many

U.S. AGENCIES RESPONSIBLE FOR NATIONAL SECURITY

The U.S. government has numerous agencies involved in protecting American citizens. Each agency has particular areas of responsibility. The Department of Homeland Security (DHS) is a cabinet-level agency, meaning it is one whose director is appointed by the president. The DHS is charged with the overall protection of America and with coordinating the response to terrorist attacks and natural disasters. The following list describes the other major agencies involved in defending America from terrorists and the role each plays:

Central Intelligence Agency (CIA): The agency responsible for gathering intelligence information on the activities of foreign terrorists, governments, and agents. The CIA focuses on threats coming from outside the United States.

Coast Guard: The organization responsible for protecting America from attacks by sea and for catching those using coastal waters to smuggle weapons and other illegal items into the country.

Department of Justice: The agency responsible for prosecuting people who commit crimes against the United States.

Federal Bureau of Investigation (FBI): A branch of the Department of Justice, the FBI is the primary organization responsible for gathering

(continued on following page)

(continued from previous page)

information on threats from domestic sources (within the United States) and investigating crimes that violate federal laws.

National Security Agency (NSA): The agency responsible for collecting and analyzing information related to foreign agents such as spies and terrorists. It is also responsible for collecting and analyzing data within the United States from communications such as telephone calls and e-mails. Its goal is to find patterns that could indicate activities that threaten the United States.

of the government's current surveillance activities are not aimed at catching specific terrorists. Instead, they scan large quantities of computerized records and numerical information, looking for patterns that may hint at terrorist activity. This process is referred to as data mining. Such widespread information gathering and analysis activities have been useful when applied by spy agencies overseas. Thus, the government is assuming that they'll be useful within the United States, as well.

The government's challenge is in figuring out how to balance the need to obtain information with the need to protect citizens from being treated unfairly. There are several issues related to widespread intelligence gathering that concern people. Is it the only effective approach—or even a good one? It is possible that there is an equally good or even better approach that would conflict less with constitutional protections. If this type of intelligence gathering is done in secret, how do we citizens protect ourselves from abuses? What happens if officials identify someone who is engaged in nonterrorist criminal activity that would not have been discovered otherwise? How do we keep the government or individual agents from using their powers against innocent people? How do we protect our right to free speech when we fear that anything we say or do could be discovered by government watchdog agencies and used against us? At what point do we cease living in a free society and find ourselves living in a police state, where all our activities are monitored?

Chapter 3

Going About Our Business

O ne of our valued freedoms is the ability to go about our daily business without interference from the government. This is one of the civil liberties granted to us by the Constitution. Prior to 9/11, this privilege was often taken for granted. Other than criminals, most people never imagined that any government agency would be interested in monitoring their day-to-day activities. Today, however, the government is using a number of surveillance tools that raise questions in the area of civil liberties. How can the government protect its citizens without making it very hard for innocent people to do normal activities, such as travel on an airplane? This chapter explores some of the tools the government is using to try to meet this challenge.

"NO-FLY" LISTS: USEFUL TOOLS OR UNREASONABLE BURDEN?

The U.S. government maintains two lists that can restrict people's ability to travel by airplane. The first is the "No-Fly" watchlist, and the second is the Automatic Selectee list. People on the No-Fly list are not allowed to board planes. People on the Automatic Selectee list are automatically chosen for detailed examination at airport security. Individuals on these lists are identified when the name on their identification matches a name in special terrorist-screening databases. The purpose of the system is to catch terrorists who are attempting to board airplanes with the intent to do harm, such as blow up or crash the plane. The system also disrupts terrorists' ability to travel, which makes it harder for them to perform coordinated acts of terror like 9/11. However, many problems have been found with the system. The greatest problem is that the data supplied by U.S. intelligence-gathering agencies is not complete or accurate. Many people have a name that is the same as the real or fake name used by a terrorist on the list. Therefore, innocent travelers have been incorrectly identified as terrorists. In addition, a report prepared by the Congressional Research Service in September 2006 indicated that the database includes numerous incorrect entries and a lot of outdated information.

The use of the watchlist has run into legal challenges both at home and abroad. In the United States, organizations like the American Civil Liberties Union (ACLU) have gone to court to try to stop the use of such systems. The ACLU is an organization whose goal is to protect the rights of American citizens. It

Rebecca Gordon *(center)* and Jan Adams *(right)* were briefly detained when their names showed up on the No-Fly list. Lawyer Jayashri Srikantiah *(standing)* is helping the women sue the U.S. government in order to reveal information about such secret lists.

claims that the collection and sharing of information on citizens who are not subjects under investigation for a specific crime is forbidden by the Constitution.

Events outside the United States have also added to the controversy. For example, the European Union had an agreement to share data on individuals for inclusion in the United States' prescreening database. In May 2006, however, the European Court of Justice canceled the agreement. Without international help, the United States cannot effectively protect its borders. Ultimately, the government is still faced with the challenge of designing and using an accurate and reliable system that

THE TERRORIST SCREENING CENTER

The Terrorist Screening Center (TSC) is the branch of the FBI charged with identifying potential terrorists. It maintains the Terrorist Screening Database (TSDB), which is a collection of data on actual and suspected international and domestic terrorists. Data in the TSDB was obtained by several government agencies. The goal of the database is to have all this information in one place, where it is accessible to law enforcement personnel. The TSC provides information to federal, state, and local law enforcement agencies.

A major issue with the TSDB is the apparent lack of accuracy of its data. If its information on suspected terrorists is incomplete, then relying on it instead of another screening method could allow terrorists to slip through the cracks. At the same time, it could cause problems if it constantly results in nonterrorists being refused the right to fly. People who say the government has violated their rights could clog up the system with claims for compensation (money paid to make up for doing harm to someone) and requests for corrections. Furthermore, past experience has shown that when a system cannot be relied upon, the staff using it eventually comes to ignore the results it produces.

protects the rights of citizens. Is it even possible for the government to develop a system that accurately identifies terrorists and doesn't make a lot of mistakes?

NATIONAL DNA DATABASE

The U.S. government plans to use high-tech scientific tools in its efforts to identify terrorists and limit their ability to do damage. For example, the U.S. Justice Department is finalizing a plan to add a DNA database to the FBI's larger crime-fighting database. DNA could be collected from:

- People arrested by government law enforcement agencies as suspects in the War on Terror
- People arrested for federal crimes (even if they are found not guilty)
- People who enter the country illegally or who stay longer than their visas allow

The total number of DNA samples could number in the hundreds of thousands. Supporters of the plan claim it will make it easier to track potential terrorists, stop illegal aliens from reentering the United States, and help solve crimes committed by illegal aliens. Opponents of the plan say collecting DNA from people who are not criminals violates people's civil liberties. They also believe it won't help stop crimes because DNA is collected from a crime scene only after the crime has already been committed. In addition, opponents point out practical problems with such a system. One is that from 2003 to 2006,

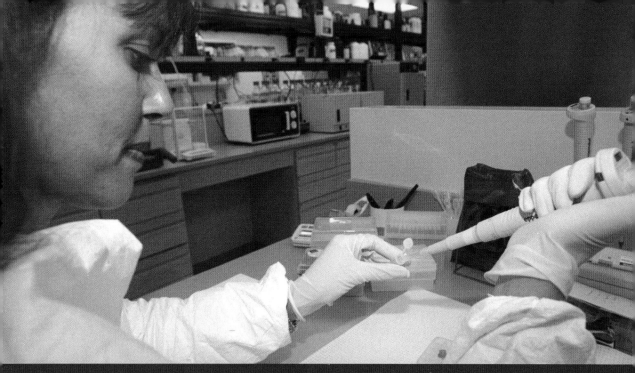

This scientist is processing a criminal's DNA. The DNA Identification Act (1994) established guidelines for a national DNA database for convicted criminals, which would be maintained by the FBI. The government now wants to expand DNA collection.

more than 400,000 illegal aliens were deported from the United States. Can we expect to analyze the DNA of each and every one of these individuals? With such a large amount of data being gathered, it is very likely that errors will occur. For example, the wrong name could be entered for a set of DNA information, or the volume of data could become so great that the database would be impossible to use.

SHOULD WE HAVE A NATIONAL IDENTITY SYSTEM?

Some suggest creating a national identity system to identify potential terrorists and track their movements. Such a program

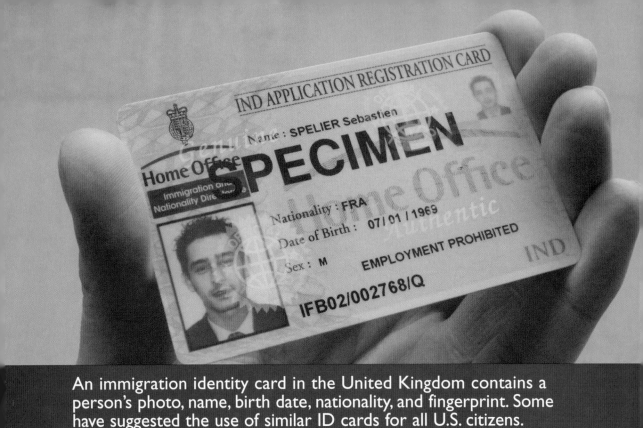

An immigration identity card in the United Kingdom contains a person's photo, name, birth date, nationality, and fingerprint. Some have suggested the use of similar ID cards for all U.S. citizens.

might include a standard identity card that could have a photo and other identifying information. The card could also possibly contain additional information on a computer chip, as the new U.S. passports do. Supporters claim that such a standardized identity system would help ensure that people are who they say they are and would make it possible to better track the movements of terrorists. Opponents say that such a system amounts to gathering intelligence on citizens who are not accused of any crime, which constitutes an invasion of privacy and is against the law.

We already show ID all the time, using state-issued driver's licenses and identification cards, student IDs, or passports to verify who we are. So why is there such a fuss? The real issue underlying the use of a national identification system is just that—it's national. The federal government would be compiling a huge database of personal information that could be used against individuals in the future. Or, if a terrorist or other criminal could hack into the database, personal information could be stolen and used for illegal purposes. Furthermore, there is a real possibility that the system will eventually require adding fingerprints, DNA data, and additional personal information to the ID to eliminate the possibility of forgery. Having all of this information available would make it even harder for individuals to protect their privacy.

Finally, there is a strong argument to be made as to whether a national identification system could even work. With modern technology, just about any document can be forged if the criminal has the means and the motivation. And in a complete system, there would be hundreds of millions of individual data files that would need to be protected. All it would take is for one terrorist to fool the system one time to pull off a deadly attack.

Chapter 4

Human Rights, the Geneva Conventions, and the War on Terror

C ivil liberties and human rights are not exactly the same. Civil liberties are rights guaranteed by law. Human rights are basic rights that all people should have. They are not necessarily guaranteed by law, but they are things that decent people agree are right. Human rights include the right to earn a living, the right not to be physically abused or cruelly punished, and the right to food and shelter. A number of human rights issues have arisen because of the U.S. government's treatment of suspected terrorists. The people held (detained) by the government as suspected terrorists are called detainees. This section looks at civil liberties and human rights issues in relation to the detainees.

DETAINING "UNLAWFUL ENEMY COMBATANTS"

Those suspected of engaging in, or supporting those engaged in, acts of terrorism have been labeled "unlawful enemy combatants" by the president. Some of these detainees are held in U.S. custody in Iraq and Afghanistan. Those who are considered especially dangerous have been held outside the United States, in secret prisons known as black sites. These detainees are held in the hopes that their long-term interrogation will lead to information that is helpful in preventing new terrorist attacks. In 2006, President Bush claimed these sites had been closed down. However, Human Rights Watch, a rights-protection group, claims that at least forty prisoners remained unaccounted for as of March 2007.

Other detainees are being held at a camp in Guantánamo Bay, Cuba. The location houses a U.S. naval base as well as the detention camp. The government chose Guantánamo Bay because it is not part of the U.S. mainland. This makes it harder for the press and other Americans to find out exactly what is going on there. In addition, it makes it difficult for people to hold protests at the site. Perhaps most important, it allows the American authorities to operate under laws different from those followed on the U.S. mainland.

DETAINEES AT GUANTÁNAMO BAY

The majority of the Guantánamo prisoners were captured abroad rather than in the United States. Former U.S. secretary of defense Donald Rumsfeld said some of the Guantánamo

detainees are undoubtedly Al Qaeda agents who were involved in active plots against Americans. As far as terrorists go, he said, these men are "the worst of the worst." However, not all of the detainees are members of terrorist organizations like Al Qaeda.

In a 2005 study, Mark Denbeaux, a professor at Seton Hall University, analyzed data on more than 500 prisoners. He found that approximately 60 percent of those detained at Guantánamo were imprisoned because they were considered "associates" of terrorists. These were people who were friends or family members of people who are alleged to support terrorist organizations. Under current law, just like those actually accused of terrorism, these people can be detained at Guantánamo for years, without access to legal help or protection.

Those who support human rights believe that the Guantánamo detainees should be treated humanely. They also believe the detainees should be tried in court within a reasonable time following their arrest. In November 2006, MSNBC.com issued a report indicating that as of the date of the report, 775 prisoners had been taken to the Guantánamo facility. However, the Pentagon's Criminal Investigation Task Force had prepared court cases against only about 100 at Guantánamo, and only

(Opposite page) Two U.S. soldiers escort a detainee at Guantánamo Bay, Cuba. A 2004 Red Cross report stated that detainees there were regularly treated in cruel and humiliating ways.

10 had actually been tried. In 2007, the Pentagon reported that approximately 390 of the detainees had been released. Others qualified for release, but officials ran into difficulty finding countries willing to comply with the U.S. government's rule that the released prisoners continue to be monitored or confined. The Pentagon claimed that approximately another 70 detainees would probably face trial. That left as many as 250 detainees who were still being held with no set date of release.

THE WRIT OF HABEAS CORPUS

Habeas corpus is a Latin term that means, literally, "you have the body." The writ (legal document) of habeas corpus basically requires the authorities to charge a prisoner with a crime or release him or her. The Sixth Amendment of the Bill of Rights states that habeas corpus is a right of U.S. citizens. It keeps the government from jailing people without just cause.

The Constitution allows the president to suspend the writ of habeas corpus in times of national emergency. Claiming that power, President George W. Bush declared that he has the right to detain individuals suspected of being terrorists "until the end of the War on Terror." But the War on Terror is not being fought against a specific enemy nation. In this way, the War on Terror is more like the U.S. government's War on Drugs than an actual military war. There is no real way to judge when the war will be over. By this logic, detainees can be held for years or decades—or forever. This raises a very basic question with regard to detainees: Do they have the right to habeas corpus and the right to challenge their detention?

A roadside demonstrator protests the treatment of detainees. In January 2007, worldwide protests marked the fifth anniversary of the arrival of the first detainees at Guantánamo Bay.

President Bush claims that keeping terrorists and their supporters out of circulation justifies a drastic action like suspending habeas corpus. However, some concerned with the safety of the American public have raised an important question: How can we know if we have actually captured the terrorists unless we bring them to trial? In court, the evidence against the defendants can be evaluated to see if they really are terrorists. Looking at the evidence gives the innocent the chance to defend themselves and also allows mistakes to be discovered. Trying all of the detainees may help us find out who and where the real terrorists are.

HABEAS CORPUS IN TIMES OF NATIONAL EMERGENCY

The U.S. president is allowed to suspend habeas corpus in times of national emergency. But what constitutes a national emergency? Should we view the threat of terrorism as an acceptable reason for suspending habeas corpus? If so, for how long? Are we willing to suspend one of our major constitutional protections for the rest of our lives? For the lives of our children or our grandchildren? If the suspension of a basic constitutional right continues for decades, will the authorities start to abuse their power? Will they begin to define domestic criminals as "domestic terrorists" and claim that the power to suspend habeas corpus applies to them? At what point will they define an act of challenging government policy as "domestic terrorism"?

The labeling of protesters as terrorists has happened before. Back in 1789, the government of the United States passed the Alien and Sedition Acts. These were four laws designed to prevent citizens of foreign countries from committing acts that could harm the U.S. government. The Alien and Sedition Acts gave the government the power to arrest and deport foreigners considered dangerous to the peace and safety of the United States. The government was allowed to imprison those who published "false, scandalous, and malicious writing" about the government or the people in it. Even back then, such government actions caused controversy. Thomas Jefferson, for example, believed they violated the Constitution and freed those imprisoned under the Alien and Sedition Acts. Similarly, during World War I, the Sedition Act of 1918 was passed specifically to outlaw government criticism while the country was at war. It was not repealed until 1921.

Without habeas corpus, will the government definitely abuse its power? Maybe not. But those who have power usually do try to hold on to it and expand it. So the question becomes: How can we protect ourselves against such abuses? One way is to pass laws that limit the time that habeas corpus can be suspended.

DO THE GENEVA CONVENTIONS APPLY TO DETAINEES OF THE WAR ON TERROR?

Conditions at the Guantánamo Bay camp are harsh. Released prisoners, such as Murat Kurnaz, a twenty-four-year-old Turkish national, claimed that he and other prisoners were subjected to torture and abuse while at the camp. Red Cross inspectors have made similar accusations. In January 2007, court records showed that FBI agents had reported various abuses to which detainees were subjected.

Many feel that tough tactics are necessary to get information from terrorists. But the treatment of prisoners at Guantánamo Bay has raised a number of human rights issues. For example, are the prisoners entitled to protections granted by the Geneva Conventions? The Geneva Conventions are four international

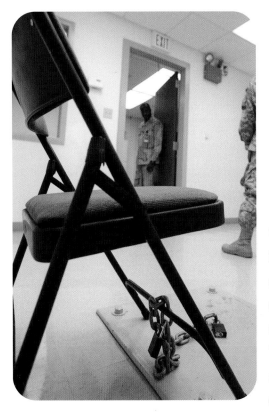

Detainees are chained to the floor in this holding room prior to being taken into the commissions room, where the U.S. military conducts its hearings for detainees.

treaties signed in Geneva, Switzerland, that detail, among other things, the way enemy soldiers and prisoners of war must be treated. (The United States signed the conventions in 1949.) For example, they outlaw the use of torture, and they require that prisoners be fed and treated humanely. They also require that prisoners be tried and sentenced by a court.

In 2001, President George W. Bush declared that detainees taken prisoner in the War on Terror are not entitled to the protections described in the Geneva Conventions. These unlawful enemy combatants, he claimed, do not represent any organization that abides by the conventions, so the Geneva protections don't apply. The president further said that if the prisoners were to be tried, it would be in military courts, which provide fewer human rights and civil liberty protections than regular U.S. criminal courts.

Chapter 5

Military Commissions, Due Process, and the Special Case of Terrorism

In June 2006, the U.S. Supreme Court ruled against President Bush, saying that trying detainees by military commissions violates both U.S. law and the Geneva Conventions. According to the Constitution, this meant that detainees had to be tried in U.S. courts. President Bush responded to the Supreme Court ruling by leading Congress to pass the Military Commissions Act of 2006. This law created courts and allowed for the use of special military commissions to try detainees. Also called military tribunals, these commissions allow secret, classified information to be used against the prisoners. The Military Commissions Act effectively returned power in this matter to the president. It also protected the CIA from having to disclose information about its treatment of detainees at the infamous black sites.

MILITARY COMMISSIONS AND SECRET COURTS

The use of military commissions to try detainees has raised many issues regarding human rights, civil liberties, and the protections afforded by the U.S. justice system. The following are some of the differences between the way cases are prosecuted in regular criminal courts and the way detainees are tried in the military commissions.

In a civilian criminal case, the accused is entitled to review all the evidence against him or her. In a military commission, the officers acting as judges can consider evidence that is kept from the accused. This, of course, affects the ability of the accused to build a defense.

In regular criminal proceedings, evidence obtained by torture is not admissible, or usable. This is not the case in the military commissions, where such evidence is allowed. On one hand, this may make it possible for interrogators (those responsible for getting information from prisoners) to obtain confessions the prisoner would otherwise refuse to make. On the other hand, this increases the chances that a prisoner will be convicted on the basis of untrue confessions made to stop the torture.

In a civilian criminal proceeding, if a prisoner is found not guilty, he or she must be released. In the case of the military commissions, the government may choose to detain a prisoner, even if the court does not find evidence of wrongdoing.

U.S. Department of Justice representatives and officers of the U.S. armed forces appear at a congressional hearing on standards for military commissions.

Our tolerance for the use of secret military commissions raises ethical issues, or issues that relate to our beliefs in what is good and bad. Which human rights, if any, are not to be violated under any circumstances? What policies, exactly, are we Americans willing to accept in the name of protecting ourselves?

DO U.S. CITIZENS HAVE SPECIAL RIGHTS?

What would happen if an American citizen was arrested as a suspected terrorist? To answer that question, we can look at the case of a detainee named José Padilla. Padilla was born in Brooklyn, New York. He adopted Islam and traveled extensively

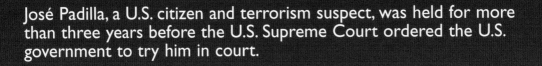

José Padilla, a U.S. citizen and terrorism suspect, was held for more than three years before the U.S. Supreme Court ordered the U.S. government to try him in court.

in the Middle East, which is heavily Muslim. Padilla was arrested at Chicago's O'Hare Airport as he came off a plane from Pakistan. He was suspected of being involved in a terrorist plot, but he was not engaged in any threatening activity at the time of his arrest. The government held him as an unlawful enemy combatant without allowing him any chance to defend himself against the charges.

The Constitution grants certain rights designed to protect American citizens from unlawful arrest and jailing. These include: the right to legal representation, the right to know the evidence against them, and the right to confront their accusers in court. These rights, along with other established legal procedures, are known as due process.

In November 2005, the Supreme Court decided that, as an American citizen, José Padilla was entitled to due process. Padilla either had to be formally charged or released. Legal proceedings related to the case were carried out during 2006, and Padilla's trial was scheduled for trial in June 2007. The importance of this ruling is not merely whether Padilla is guilty. The bigger issue is whether American citizens can be held indefinitely without trial because the government thinks they are dangerous. The answer was a long time in coming, but it finally came down on the side of the Constitution: American citizens accused of any crime, including terrorism, are entitled due process, the right to defend themselves in court, and a timely trial.

SHOULD DETAINEES HAVE THE RIGHT TO DUE PROCESS?

One argument that has been used to justify the suspension of individual rights is that terrorism is a crime in a class by itself, so it requires a different legal approach. Our entire legal system is based on the idea that a person is innocent until proven guilty. Another way to say this is: "It is better to occasionally let a crook go free than to imprison a single innocent person." However, there are those who believe that a single terrorist act can do such great harm that a different standard should be applied: "Better to let some innocent people be imprisoned unfairly than to let a single terrorist slip through the cracks." There are two potential problems with this approach: First, how many people is "some"? And second, at what point are more people suffering at the hands of the government than would be harmed by the terrorists?

Arriving at an answer to this question is not easy. Everyone remembers the devastation of 9/11, but not so many think about the thousands of people whose loved ones have been jailed, many unjustly. This leads people to dismiss both the danger and pain of the latter experience.

The proper way to address the problem of fair treatment of detainees is not necessarily an either/or situation. Rather, it may require taking another look at the different types of prisoners. In other words, it is reasonable to treat an individual captured at an Al Qaeda training camp differently from a humanitarian aid worker providing food in a remote region that may contain terrorists.

There may be times when the evidence that a person is a terrorist comes from an undercover agent or informant. It's true that revealing the name of that informant may put his or her life at risk and interfere with other ongoing investigations. However, it's also true that in most cases, the person in question will not be in that position forever. Furthermore, it is quite possible that a reasonable compromise could be worked out. It may be possible to protect the identity of the source while still allowing a suspect to present evidence that he or she is not involved in terrorism. This is different from the way things are done in regular court cases, where a suspect can see all the evidence against him or her. But, for the defendant, having some information withheld while still being able to present evidence that one is innocent is better than not having the opportunity to defend oneself at all.

This is a view from the air of the former site of the World Trade Center in New York City. Even as the site is rebuilt, the United States struggles with the legacy of the terrorist attacks of September 11, 2001.

Another option would be for Congress to limit the time during which the president may suspend habeas corpus. For example, he could be allowed to suspend habeas corpus for two years. After that, Congress would have to approve another two years. In that way, legislators representing the public could decide whether a state of emergency still exists. Or they could decide that the threat is no longer so great that such extraordinary measures are necessary.

Chapter 6

Has the War on Terror Made Us Safer?

Many wonder if the government's approach is the best way to address the terrorist threat. The problem with this question is that no one knows the answer. The government claims it can make Americans safer but that it must possibly violate some civil liberties in the process. However, the question remains: Are the measures the government is taking making us safer than measures it could take that do not violate civil liberties?

IS THE GOVERNMENT'S WAY THE BEST WAY?

The government has presented its plan as the best alternative to leaving ourselves open to attack by terrorists.

Part of that plan is the continuing war in Iraq. By creating a war front overseas, the Bush administration feels that it has kept terrorists from focusing on the United States. This may help protect the human rights of us Americans, but Iraqi human rights have not fared as well.

In a war zone, there is only so much that can be done to protect people's human rights and civil liberties. On the home front, however, we have more control over our actions. In this light, surveillance, detention, and prosecution do not necessarily have to be viewed as a matter of "all or nothing." It is possible for the government to carry on its activities under clearer regulations and with greater oversight. Judges could be given the task of reviewing government activities more carefully. This would be less convenient for the government, but it would not stop agents from monitoring suspected terrorists' communications, for example. What it would do is reduce the chance that the government could abuse the vast powers granted to it under the Patriot Act.

DOES FEWER CIVIL LIBERTIES EQUAL GREATER SAFETY?

This is another question that can't be answered with certainty. In the days immediately following the terrorist attacks of 9/11, the Patriot Act was rushed into law. The president and, especially, the vice president, pushed Congress to approve it. There was no time for a thorough analysis of the U.S. intelligence-gathering system. Nor was there any attempt to analyze exactly why the existing system allowed the terrorists to pull off their attacks in the first place. As a result, the government made some broad assumptions without figuring out the specific problems or alternative ways to address them. Nor did the government include any way to review the measures, once they were put in place.

Because the legislation had to be rushed, we ended up with no sure way of knowing if the activities are actually benefiting us. There have been no new large-scale terrorist attacks on America since the measures were taken. But large-scale terrorists attacks on America were rare events throughout history. The fact that no such attacks have occurred in the years since does not necessarily mean that attacks were stopped. Terrorist attacks may take years to plan, and it is possible that no such events were attempted. This makes it all the more important that we catch the right people.

The issue of the collection of huge quantities of data on Americans goes beyond the question of protecting citizens' civil liberties. It's also a matter of protecting their lives. The collection of vast quantities of data with no clear target in mind other than "finding something suspicious" does not necessarily make us safer. We have huge volumes of data piling up, waiting to be analyzed. Is this more useful than focusing on tips or evidence that specific individuals are engaged in a dangerous activity? Is the important clue about a particular terrorist lost somewhere in a mountain of data? Are there better ways to locate potential terrorists? Questions like these should make us wonder if it would make sense to go back to the drawing board and reanalyze the situation. With a fresh perspective, we may be able to find a better approach to locating potential terrorists, with less disruption of our civil liberties.

RESPONSE TO THE U.S TREATMENT OF DETAINEES

At home and abroad, the U.S. government's treatment of detainees has been harshly criticized. A BBC World Service survey completed in January 2007 showed that 67 percent of 26,381 respondents from 25 countries said they disapproved of the way in which the United States was handling the detainees at Guantánamo. The activities at Guantánamo Bay have caused conflict with other nations and international organizations, whose cooperation is needed if the United States is to succeed in controlling terrorist activities. The United Nations, the European Union, and Amnesty International all have requested that the United States close down the Guantánamo prison.

By the middle of 2007, even members of the U.S. Senate were calling for change. For example, on April 27, 2007, Senator Carl Levin told the Senate Armed Services Committee, "America at its best is a beacon for

Demonstrators gather in front of the American embassy in London in January 2007 as part of an Amnesty International protest.

(continued on following page)

(continued from previous page)

human rights and human liberty, and that's how we like to see ourselves. But much of the world sees us in a very different way when we fail to live up to the standards we profess. For us, the symbol of American values is the Statue of Liberty. For much of the world, it is that horrific photograph of a hooded prisoner at Abu Ghraib, standing on a box, strung up with wires."

STRIKING A BALANCE BETWEEN LIBERTY AND TYRANNY

As we have seen, one of the toughest issues that we face today is how to deal with the threat of terrorism. President George W. Bush has chosen to characterize the issue of terrorism as a war. But is the threat from terrorists really a war?

The danger we face is not the sort that results from a hostile country storming our shores, as was the case when Japan bombed Pearl Harbor, requiring our entry into World War II. A case can be made that the situation is more like the Cold War with the Soviet Union that lasted from the 1950s to 1991. The Cold War was so-called because the two superpowers never directly engaged in warfare.

Senator Joseph McCarthy *(center)* speaks during a 1954 congressional hearing. At a time when Communism appeared to represent the greatest threat to America, McCarthy accused thousands of Americans of being Communists or supporting them.

During much of this period, however, Americans truly believed that the Communist Soviet Union might launch a nuclear attack on the United States at any moment. Because of the perceived threat, U.S. intelligence agencies had an urgent need to gather and analyze intelligence data. The government actively pursued suspected Communists, investigating not just those in the government but in all walks of life.

In the 1950s, Senator Joseph McCarthy demanded that Congress hold hearings to try to identify prominent Communists. These hearings ultimately led to the blacklisting of thousands of Americans with ties—even weak ties—to the Communist Party in the United States. When people were blacklisted, their names were placed on a list, and no one would hire them or help them for fear that they, too, would be labeled a Communist. Most Americans look back on these events in our history as a terrible mistake. Blacklisting trampled civil liberties and ruined the lives of many people.

IN CONCLUSION

In this new age of terrorism, the question we are faced with is: "Will we repeat the mistakes of the past, or will we learn from them?" It is true that we cannot ignore the terrorist threat and end up with bombs exploding in our crowded cities. But we must also make sure that our attempts to keep Americans safe do not end up ruining people's lives. We must come up with a balanced approach that preserves civil liberties and allows people to feel secure from unjustified attacks by the government as well as from terrorists.

Timeline

February 26, 1993 Under orders by Osama bin Laden, four terrorists set off a car bomb under the World Trade Center in New York, killing 6 and injuring 100.

April 19, 1995 Timothy McVeigh sets off a car bomb in front of a federal building in Oklahoma City, killing 168 and injuring 600.

1996 The Antiterrorism and Effective Death Penalty Act is passed; it contains many provisions later incorporated into the Patriot Act.

July 1996 A bomb set off at a concert during the Atlanta Olympics kills 2 and injures 110.

August 1998 Terrorist bombings of U.S. embassies in Nairobi, Kenya, and Dar es Salaam, Tanzania, leave 263 dead and 5,000 injured.

October 2000 Terrorists bomb the USS *Cole* in the Yemeni port of Aden, killing 17.

September 11, 2001 Terrorists attack World Trade Center in New York, and the Pentagon, outside Washington, D.C.

September 20, 2001 President George W. Bush creates the Office of Homeland Security.

September 26, 2001 The USA PATRIOT Act is signed into law.

2001 A military prison camp is established at the U.S. naval base at Guantánamo Bay, Cuba, to house foreign nationals suspected of being involved in terrorism. The treatment of prisoners there draws criticism in the United States and abroad.

November 25, 2002 The Homeland Security Act of 2002 makes the Department of Homeland Security a cabinet-level agency of the U.S. government.

January 29, 2003 The American Library Association issues a resolution stating its belief that certain sections of the Patriot Act violate the constitutional and privacy rights of library patrons.

January 23, 2004 The Supreme Court makes its first ruling against a provision in the Patriot Act when it rules in favor of the Humanitarian Law Project, stating that classifying "giving expert advice or assistance" as terrorism violates the First and Fifth Amendments.

September 30, 2004 The Supreme Court rules in favor of the ACLU, declaring unconstitutional the requirement in the Patriot Act that Internet service providers turn over records to the FBI on presentation of National Security Letters, which don't require a court order.

April 6, 2005 Senators Larry Craig (R-ID), John Sununu (R-NH), and Richard Durbin (D-IL) propose the Security and Freedom Enhancement Act, which would place safeguards on the powers granted by the Patriot Act.

January 1, 2006 The U.S. government agrees to pay $200,000 to settle a lawsuit brought by the ACLU over the No-Fly list.

March 9, 2006 The Patriot Act is reauthorized for another three years.

June 19, 2006 The U.S. Supreme Court declares that prisoners held in Guantánamo Bay are protected by the Geneva Conventions, an international set of rules that govern how prisoners of war must be treated.

September 2006 U.S. Congress passes the Military Commissions Act, authorizing the use of military tribunals to try detainees.

May 2007 May 2007 Federal trial begins for José Padilla, an American citizen accused of conspiring to aid Al Qaeda terrorists.

June 2007 U.S. military tribunal judges dismiss war crimes charges against two Guantánamo detainees, ruling that the military had not followed procedures to declare the detainees "unlawful enemy combatants," a requirement for the military tribunal to hear the case.

2009 The Patriot Act is scheduled for reauthorization.

Glossary

alias A false name used to disguise a person's real identity.

Al Qaeda A major Mideast-based terrorist organization whose goal is to disrupt Western countries.

Bill of Rights Ten amendments added to the U.S. Constitution that spell out rights guaranteed to Americans.

compensation Money paid to a person to make up for injury or suffering.

data mining Collecting and analyzing large amounts of data to find patterns.

DNA Deoxyribonucleic acid; the material that encodes our genetic characteristics. Each person's DNA is unique.

due process The applying of the law in such a way that a person is not denied his or her rights and is in line with basic accepted legal principles.

illegal alien Someone who enters the country from a foreign nation without being granted permission.

intelligence Information gathered and analyzed to find clues to significant activity.

legislation Laws proposed or passed by Congress.

seizure Capture or arrest.

surveillance Watching and monitoring someone's activities.

tribunal Special military court sometimes set up to try crimes committed during wartime.

For More Information

American Civil Liberties Union
125 Broad Street
New York, NY 10004
Web site: http://www.aclu.org

Amnesty International
5 Penn Plaza, 14th Floor
New York, NY 10001
Web site: http://www.amnestyusa.org

Central Intelligence Agency (CIA)
Office of Public Affairs
Washington, DC 20505
Web site: http://www.cia.gov

Electronic Privacy Information Center
1718 Connecticut Avenue NW, Suite 200
Washington, DC 20009
Web site: http://www.epic.org

Federal Bureau of Investigation (FBI)
J. Edgar Hoover Building
935 Pennsylvania Avenue NW
Washington, DC 20535-0001
Web site: http://www.fbi.gov

League of Women Voters
1730 M Street NW, Suite 1000
Washington, DC 20036-4508
Web site: http://www.lwv.org

U.S. Department of Homeland Security
Washington, DC 20528
Web site: http://www.dhs.gov

U.S. Department of Justice
950 Pennsylvania Avenue NW
Washington, DC 20530-0001
Web site: http://www.usdoj.gov

U.S. Department of State
2201 C Street NW
Washington, DC 20520
Web site: http://www.usinfo.state.gov/is/international_security/
    terrorism.html

WEB SITES

Due to the changing nature of Internet links, Rosen Publishing
has developed an online list of Web sites related to the subject
of this book. This site is updated regularly. Please use this link
to access the list:

http://www.rosenlinks.com/ad/adcl

For Further Reading

Frank, Mitch. *Understanding September 11: Answering Questions About the Attack on America*. New York, NY: Viking, 2002.

Freedman, Jeri. *America Debates Privacy vs. Security*. New York, NY: Rosen Publishing, 2008.

Friedman, Laurie S. *Introducing Issues with Opposing Viewpoints: Terrorism*. Chicago, IL: Greenhaven Press, 2005.

Gerdes, Louise I. *The Patriot Act*. Chicago, IL: Greenhaven Press, 2005.

Hudson, David L., Jr. *Open Government: An American Tradition Faces National Security, Privacy, and Other Challenges*. New York, NY: Chelsea House, 2005.

McCgwire, Scarlett, and Paul Dowsdell. *Surveillance: The Impact on Our Lives*. Chicago, IL: Raintree, 2001.

Nakaya, Andrea C. *Current Controversies: Homeland Security*. Chicago, IL: Greenhaven Press, 2004.

New York Times. *The Nation Challenged*. New York, NY: Scholastic Reference, 2002.

Ojeda, Auriana. *Civil Liberties*. Chicago, IL: Greenhaven Press, 2004.

Torr, James. *Civil Liberties and the War on Terrorism*. Chicago, IL: Lucent Books, 2004.

Bibliography

Ackerman, Bruce. *Before the Next Attack: Preserving Civil Liberties in an Age of Terrorism*. New Haven, CT: Yale University Press, 2006.

Babington, Charles, and Michael Abramowitz. "U.S. Shifts Policy on Geneva Conventions." *Washington Post*, July 12, 2006.

Cole, David, and James X. Dempsey. *Terrorism and the Constitution*. New York, NY: The New Press, 2006.

Dedman, Bill. "In Limbo: Cases Are Few Against Gitmo Detainees." MSNBC.com. October 24, 2006. Retrieved February 2, 2007 (http://www.msnbc.msn.com/id/15361740).

Dempsey, James X. "Civil Liberties in a Time of Terror." *Human Rights*. Retrieved December 28, 2006 (http://www.abanet.org/irr/hr/winter02/dempsey.html).

Federal Bureau of Investigation. "Counterterrorism—Terrorist Screening Center." Retrieved March 2, 2007 (http://www.fbi.gov/terrorinfo/counterterrorism/faqs.htm).

Krouse, William J., and Bart Elias. "CRS Report for Congress: Terrorist Watchlist Checks and Air Passenger Prescreening." Washington, DC: Congressional Research Service/Library of Congress, September 6, 2006.

Darmer, M. Katherine B., Robert M. Baird, and Stuart E. Rosenbaum, eds. *Civil Liberties vs. National Security in a Post-9/11 World*. Amherst, NY: Prometheus Books, 2004.

Leone, Richard C., and Greg Anrig Jr., eds. *The War on Our Freedoms: Civil Liberties in an Age of Terrorism*. New York, NY: Public Affairs, 2003.

Bibliography

World Public Opinion.org. "Americans Support Full Due-Process
  Rights for Terrorism Suspects." July 17, 2006. Retrieved
  February 10, 2007 (http://www.worldpublicopinion.org/pipa/
  articles/home_page/228.php?nid=&id=&pnt=228&lb=hmpg).

Index

Index

ABOUT THE AUTHOR

Jeri Freedman has a B.A. from Harvard University. She is the author of other nonfiction books published by Rosen Publishing, including *Primary Sources in American History: Colonies—Massachusetts* and *America Debates Privacy vs. Security*. Under the name Ellen Foxxe, she is the coauthor of two alternate history science fiction novels. She lives in Boston.

PHOTO CREDITS

Designer: Gene Mollica; **Editor:** Christopher Roberts
Photo Researcher: Cindy Reiman